They Call It Church Hurt

Volume 1
Church People

PADRIKA GRAY

ISBN-13: 978-0-9996130-0-9

LCCN: 2017917802

Edited by October Day Publishing
www.octoberdaypublishing.pub

Note: The word "offense" in The King James Version of the Bible, is spelled "offence". Only the King James Version scripture quotations containing this word will be spelled in that manner.

CONTENTS

Introduction

You have offended me! It's an unavoidable part of human nature, however, not excusable as such. Is it possible not to offend? Few have mastered it. The idea that physical objects can hurt a person more than an unkind word sounds good, but is not accurate. Death and life are in the power of the tongue (Proverbs 18:21 KJV). Speaking the wrong words can potentially destroy a person emotionally, cause physical ailments and other medical symptoms.

What if the church was like a hospital? What if it received people from all walks of life—people who bring their baggage with them, hoping to stay a while, each one looking for healing and to resolve the issues of life? Some respond to treatment; some don't. Some accept the prescription or answer provided; some reject it and look for a second opinion. Using this analogy, can you imagine why an offensive encounter is inevitable in the church?

At the end of each chapter, an Affirmation, Reading & Meditation section "Strength for the Journey," with space for journaling, is provided for self-study. These tools will empower and strengthen the resolve of those who are determined to grow in God's grace; and while doing so, have experienced the effects or after-effects of wounds and hurts in their interactions with other Believers. My intention is not to tear down, accuse, or embarrass the institution of the church or its members, but purely to identify with those who still need care and share some of the things I have learned. To my brothers and sisters who are still hurting in this area, "I understand!" and so does the Father God, your creator.

It is vital we learn how to navigate and quickly recover from offenses. In the spirit of meekness, I pray these books will facilitate the healing process, restore trust, and ultimately the return of those who have previously decided to forsake the church congregation because of what they call: Church Hurt.

Strength for the Journey

Affirmation - Healing:
I admit that I have received an offense in church, and that I have offended others. I quickly and freely forgive. I confess that I have not been offended by God; I am confident that he understands and loves me. I will thank Him daily for being my help and strength. I open my heart now to receive healing and deliverance in this area.

Reading & Meditation:
Woe unto the world because of offences! For it must needs be that offences come; but woe to that man by whom the offence cometh! (Matthew 18:7 KJV)

For in many things we offend all. If any man offend not in word, the same is a perfect man, and able also to bridle the whole body. (James 3:2 KJV);

"And the times of this ignorance God winked at; but now commandeth all men every where to repent..."
(Acts 17:30 KJV)

And the second is like, namely this, Thou shalt love thy neighbour as thyself. There is none other commandment greater than these. (Mark 12:31 KJV)

For we have not an high priest which cannot be touched with the feeling of our infirmities; but was in all points tempted like as we are, yet without sin. (Hebrews 4:15 KJV)

Journal
Healing from Offense

_____

_____

_____

_____

_____

_____

_____

_____

_____

_____

_____

_____

_____

_____

_____

_____

_____

_____

_____

_____

_____

_____

_____

Why Fellowship?

It can't be denied. Many people have proclaimed, "I've been hurt in church," and now believe in limiting their fellowship with the intention of minimizing the inevitable offense. The Bible talks about using wisdom in our interactions with family, friends and acquaintances to circumvent wearing out one's welcome. However, it is still important that we understand the role we play as Believers co-laboring together. Confidence in this area could significantly reduce offenses.

Every person should expect to be cared for and appreciated. In our physical bodies, notice how the heart and hand perform in support of almost every part of the body, while the foot has a few specific ministries (as with the eye and the nose), but they each work in one accord to ensure the body functions properly. No part of the physical body is considered less important because of its primary or secondary role.

There are people with multiple talents; some have one gift or one talent. Whatever the number, they were given by God for a purpose. An example of how offenses happen during church fellowship is when the individual with many talents is expected to be self-debasing (to decrease in quality, status or character) in order not to offend those whose gifts or talents are not on display. Self-debasement is not rooted in love, it is rooted in "fear" of hurting someone's feelings, rather than glorifying God and letting Him work through an individual in support of the church. How can anyone perform efficiently with the gifts or talents God has given if they are afraid of how someone will react? God never said the one with many gifts and talents is better than the one with few; only that we should glorify Him with what He has given us, which leaves no room for self-exaltation. I believe if we do what the scripture says, and esteem others better than ourselves, there may be fewer instances of low self-worth and offenses in our churches.

Sometimes "I can do that better!" is the attitude of Believers whose gifts or talents have not been revealed. If rooted in competition, this mentality creates chaos. Teamwork directed toward God's purpose will ensure the church is equipped to teach and empower, not compete for recognition. Think about how the heart works in our physical bodies. It pumps life-giving blood to places where the foot and eye could never go. Wouldn't some part of your physical body fail (or be offended) if your eye tried to do what your heart does? If the heart is offended, it will threaten to shut down because of that offense; this analogy holds true in our interactions with people in the church.

Along with having fun and enjoying life, healthy fellowship involves showing respect for each other's differences, praying effectually and fervently for one other; esteeming others better than ourselves, genuine love, and communicating with diplomacy. When fellowship is incorrect, people will witness and sometimes be a party to different displays of dishonesty and disobedience, which includes murmuring, gossiping, backbiting, sedition, and heresy (enticement to rebel, opposition, and dispute). When we set our affections on things that are pleasing to God, not only will we display integrity (decency, honor, morality, respect, reliability, uprightness), but we maintain proper fellowship with God.

If your gift or talent has not been revealed, continue to pray. While you are waiting in faith, fully investigate the things and issues that tug at your heart. Your gifts might be hidden in an issue you care deeply about or something you love to do. Also, don't neglect to counsel with your Pastor or other designated leader. Refuse to hide out or avoid being around people on a continual basis to lessen your chances of offending, or being offended. Separation for consecration is necessary but does not negate the need for fellowship which promotes unity, communication, brotherly love, and sharing of our gifts and talents to strengthen the church.

Strength for the Journey

Affirmation - Love:
Today, I will pray about the God kind of love and make a conscious effort to show it to anyone who I believe has offended me. I will ask for and use wisdom in all my relationships and strive to be kind and tender-hearted.

Reading & Meditation:
Withdraw thy foot from thy neighbor's house; lest he be weary of thee, and so hate thee. (Proverbs 25:17 KJV)

There is no fear in love; but perfect love casteth out fear: because fear hath torment. He that feareth is not made perfect in love. (I John 4:18 KJV)

"And let us consider one another to provoke unto love and to good works: Not forsaking the assembling of ourselves together, as the manner of some is..." (Hebrews 10:24-25 KJV)

Affirmation – Your Gifts & Talents:
I am neither over qualified nor under qualified. I will be patient, prepared, and in place when God calls for my gift in the church. I will pray that those who are currently yielding their gifts continue to do so with integrity.

Reading & Meditation:
Let nothing be done through strife or vainglory; but in lowliness of mind let each esteem others better than themselves. (Philippians 2:3 KJV)

"For I say through the grace given unto me, to every man that is among you, not to think of himself more highly than he ought to think; but to think soberly, according as God has dealt to every man the measure of faith..." (Romans 12:3-5 KJV)

Journal
Why Fellowship?

_____

_____

_____

_____

_____

_____

_____

_____

_____

_____

_____

_____

_____

_____

_____

_____

_____

_____

_____

_____

_____

_____

_____

_____

_____

A Brother Offended - A Sister Offended

The Truth is: There is a chance that good relationship may never be restored to its original state. "A brother offended is harder to be won than a strong city: and their contentions are like the bars of a castle" (Proverbs 18:19 KJV). It may be difficult not to offend, but not impossible. As we develop our relationship with God, and move into different levels of maturity and obedience, certain aspects of our spiritual growth may require that we spontaneous leap out of a situation that produces death, into one that creates life. No one can determine the speed at which another person is growing in their faith. When a relationship severs because of another person's desire to repent, obey, or pursue their dreams, there is bound to be contention. The act of separating can provoke anger, resentment, bitterness, rejection, self-justification, backbiting, tale-bearing, jealousy, just to name a few; but hopefully, true repentance leading to deliverance will take precedence over all. Obeying God's

Word involves separation from the source or spirit of disobedience. The part that often makes this act of obedience difficult is dealing with people, their will, their emotions and their opinions; all of which should be put under subjection. Nothing spiritually significant gets accomplished until we surrender our will to God in obedience.

Often, we think our actions are spirit-led until change, flexibility, and obedience become difficult. We feel that pain, immediately reject it and in the heat of the moment, respond inappropriately. The Book of Proverbs says, "Let a bear robbed of her whelps [babies] meet a man, [rather] than a fool his folly" (Proverbs 17:2 KJV). Can you imagine the rage of a mother bear whose babies were taken? The Book of Proverbs relates that anger to a man or woman confronted with their faults. Confrontation brings resolution, but it must be done correctly. Until you are skilled in the process, solicit the support of a mediator. Broken fellowship and genuine love in your relationships can be restored. It can be done prayerfully, with wisdom, and without placing yourself in the same unhealthy predicament knowing the facts. The goal is peace and cohesiveness [unity and teamwork].

When something must be done in the earth, God requires the cooperation a human being. He allows us to continue functioning in the church with our gifts, many times with our faults showing. Those gifts and callings of God were given to us without our repentance, before we were born; some are revealed after we are "born again". Remember, never simply write off anyone because they have caused or received an offense. That individual may be carrying within them something that God has designed (or is preparing) to bless another individual or to strengthen the Kingdom. Reconciliation and retention may be hard after an offense; but recovery is not impossible.

Strength for the Journey

Affirmation:
I remember a situation where I lost my focus and became enraged with my brother or sister in church. I commit to pray about my temper until it is subdued. I can do this. I trust God's anointing to do the rest. My gifts and talents will operate in a greater capacity when I am delivered from the bondage of anger.

Reading & Meditation:
A brother offended is harder to be won than a strong city: and their contentions are like the bars of a castle.
(Proverbs 18:19 KJV)

For the Word of God is quick, and powerful, and sharper than any two-edged sword, piercing even to the dividing asunder of soul and spirit, and of the joints and marrow, and is a discerner of the thoughts and intents of the heart.
(Hebrews 4:12 KJV)

Let a bear robbed of her whelps meet a man, than a fool his folly. (Proverbs 17:12 KJV)

And it shall come to pass in that day, that his burden shall be taken away from off thy shoulder, and his yoke from off thy neck, and the yoke shall be destroyed because of the anointing. (Isaiah 10:27 KJV)

For the gifts and calling of God are without repentance.
(Romans 11:29 KJV)

Journal
A Brother Offended, A Sister Offended

Are You A Fighter?

If you are easily provoked, your real adversary (the devil) knows it, and he will make an extra effort to pick a fight with your emotions. There is a time for confrontation, and a proper way to confront another Believer, but seek Godly counsel first. No encounter with people should be an immediate impulse of the flesh responding to an emotionally charged situation. The mind can create full-color action videos, complete with sound, that suggest a situation happened one way, and demand you accept it as truth; when it is false. If your flesh reacts to what you've visualized, and you add dynamite to the fire that is already blazing in your mind, there's going to be an explosion. You'll be at the point of no return and, no doubt, it will require much prayer to keep you from backsliding. Are you willing to take that chance? It may initially be uncomfortable, but we can accomplish more when we are controlling our emotions than we can by acting out what feels good to the flesh. The flesh provides immediate and false gratification which comes with a price. I found out: The same situation handled correctly through spiritual warfare and obedience to God's Word brings life, peace, and deliverance. Never be excited about paying your enemies back. Trusting God to handle something that you want to fix yourself takes faith; and without faith, it is impossible to please God. Don't let the devil use "church people" to provoke you into sin. Fight the right way. Be free-hearted with forgiveness and mercy, and let the Lord fight your battles.

Now if you want to intentionally retaliate, go into your secret prayer closet, and don't tell anyone. Pray and intercede for your fellow Believer who has a problem with fornication and lust. Fighting with smart remarks and criticism only pushes people further away from God. Fight for the Believer who is experiencing feelings of rejection, depression, and oppression. Pray and intercede for your fellow Believer who wants a wife or a husband, but lacks wisdom concerning the process. Don't laugh and make jokes at their inabilities, and later find yourself I the same predicament. Pray for the Pastors and leaders who have been called to teach and empower. Fight in the spirit for their protection from the enemies of their soul, for their physical health, pray about the vision and strength of the church, and for all Pastors to experience a continual fresh anointing to preach the Word of God to their congregations in power and authority. Pray and fight "for" them in the spirit, not against them. Stand in the gap for others and do battle in prayer so the Lord will prepare each person spiritually to receive the answers they desire. Pray the Lord's will be accomplished in their lives, whatever the outcome.

If you are a fighter, direct your energy against the devil. Instead of fighting against flesh and blood, put those skills to good use in the Kingdom of God as you fight and do battle against the forces of darkness with the Word of God!

Strength for the Journey

Affirmation:
I acknowledge that I have some fight in me either from birth or from circumstances that forced me to grow up a certain way. I will ask God for wisdom when I feel my flesh rising and I will not immediately act when I am offended. I understand that I am not wrestling with the church or its members. I will obtain strength from the Word of God to direct my fight toward the enemy of my soul, and I will win.

Reading & Meditation:
Not rendering evil for evil, or railing for railing: but contrariwise blessing; knowing that ye are thereunto called, that ye should inherit a blessing. (1 Peter 3:9 KJV)

Rejoice not when thine enemy falleth, and let not thine heart be glad when he stumbleth: Lest the Lord see it, and it displease him, and he turn away his wrath from upon him. (Proverbs 24:17-18 KJV)

"He that handleth a matter wisely shall find good: ..." (Proverbs 16:20)

For the weapons of our warfare are not carnal, but mighty through God to the pulling down of strong holds; Casting down imaginations, and every high thing that exalteth itself against the knowledge of God, and bringing into captivity every thought to the obedience of Christ; And having in a readiness to revenge all disobedience, when your obedience is fulfilled. (II Corinthians 10:4-6 KJV)

For we wrestle not against flesh and blood, but against principalities, against powers, against the rulers of the darkness of this world, against spiritual wickedness in high places. (Ephesians 6:12 KJV)

Journal
Are You A Fighter?

Is Your Struggle With People?

Have you ever thought the world would be a better place to live if everyone had the same personality as you? Someone may be laughing right now; but many have secretly amused themselves with that thought or something like it. I can imagine they've said, "I'm a reasonably rational and sound minded person; I pay my bills on time; I have a house, car and a money market account." Some may have thought, "I have successful friends and a secure job; I don't say senseless things to get attention; what's wrong with other people?"

The things that are different about each of us is what makes us stronger together. Some parts of our character are present at birth, handed down through generations; and some learned from the environments that we grow up in, past and present. In any event, we've all been designed to complement each other. We are called the Body of Christ; therefore, every part is essential, and each of them performs an essential role. Our toes are the smallest digits on our bodies; yet, without them, it can be difficult to balance and walk. They work in sync with our feet. Our eyes are important. If darkness suddenly overtakes them, our hands immediately reach out for safety, and our other senses pitch in to help with stabilization.

If you've mastered a certain thing in your character or personality, and it is no longer problematic, be kind and patient with other Believers who appear not to have reached that level. You may know a person who appears distracted or confused about the role they play in the church. They may have lost focus because they saw you doing something that appeared to be more interesting. Now, they not only want to do what you're doing, but they also want to receive recognition for work prepared in advance of their grand entrance. According to the Bible, we should not boast about things in any area where our hands have made no prior preparations. So, to cover the transgression with love, you've concluded the individual is only trying to figure out what he or she does well. But, your aggravation with their confusion and what seems like their attempts to take over your role, is undeniable. Whatever the situation, kindness should be one of the attributes shown, not defensiveness, impatience or annoyance. Make every attempt to keep the atmosphere peaceful. Consider this: That person has crossed your path because God trusts you to pray for them, not kill their spirit. Pray the spirit of jealousy and covetousness doesn't overtake them while they wait on God to reveal or release them to perform in their gifts or talents. Pray their self-worth and faith are not frustrated and that God will direct and guide their lives. In your private prayer time, rebuke the spirit of pride, high-mindedness and other uncooperative spirits. Later, when God's gifts and talents are in action, there will be no division in the church. Treat people the way you would like to be treated and repent daily. Consider yourself, lest you also be tempted in the same manner!

Strength for the Journey

Affirmation:
I will intentionally pray that my eyes be opened, and I am able to see the many ways that we complement each other in the church with our gifts, talents, and with our personalities. I will keep the right spirit, stay in my lane, and walk in peace inside and outside of the church.

Reading & Meditation:
"Be kindly affectioned one to another with brotherly love; in honour preferring one another...". (Romans 12:10 KJV)

For the body is not one member, but many. If the foot shall say, because I am not the hand, I am not of the body; is it therefore not of the body? (1 Corinthians 12:14-15 KJV)

"...and not to boast in another man's line of things made ready to our hand...". (2 Corinthians 10:16 KJV)

If it be possible, as much as lieth in you, live peaceably with all men. (Romans 12:18 KJV)

Brethren, if a man be overtaken in a fault, ye which are spiritual, restore such an one in the spirit of meekness; considering thyself, lest thou also be tempted. (Galatians 6:1 KJV)

Journal
Is Your Struggle With People?

Keep Your Eyes Off Church People

In the late 1990's, I held a conversation with a teenager who was trying to live Godly. He grew up in church and had befriended a few people (his peers); he just didn't fit into their clique. The path that his life was taking also appeared to be different; yet, he still wanted to be accepted. Who doesn't want acceptance somewhere or someplace in their lifetime? He grew into a young adult, and life quickly pulled him in several different directions. As he continued to activate and maneuver in the power of his own will, he wondered whether he was serving God because of what he was taught to do under parental supervision or of his own free will. Handling his own affairs and learning to live life as an independent adult introduced him to more people than those whom he knew in church. These people accepted him (or sincerely pretended to), and the church people for whatever reason isolated him. How do you keep the spirit of rejection from taking root? How do you not conform to that group of "church people" who are existing in a clique and struggling to live right? This young man went through several other phases in his life; and ultimately, he learned that it was okay to stand alone. He didn't become bitter about the rejection he experienced in his past or even his present. He stood firm against the pressure to conform to the wrong group or the wrong thing. I can't say that he never failed; but he always triumphed. This young man learned how to communicate with God; the one who knows all and still wants to dialogue with us about whatever concerns us.

Don't get me wrong; not one of us who knows anything about God can make the excuse that they fell into sin because of someone else. But thank God for Jesus! He is our mediator. When we confess our faults, we are quickly forgiven and cleansed from all unrighteousness. There will be many occasions when we must stand alone, against the pressure to conform. Consider it another opportunity to develop a closer relationship with your God and to sharpen your spiritual weapons.

Great things and great deliverance are birthed through prayer and persistence. Stay focused on the prize—Heaven, eternal life! Don't spend lots of time watching the negative behavior of others while they are growing and developing. Pay attention to what you have been instructed to do and to become. God will deal with His children who have allowed themselves to become a stumbling block to others. Each one of us is expected to work out our own salvation. We cannot control the actions of others, and we must not write anyone off. God has given each of us a will along with the tools and the ability to choose wisely or poorly. Therefore, choose life, and if you want to live (for Christ) keep your eyes off church people!

Strength for the Journey

Affirmation:
Father God, thank you for helping me stay focused and to make the right choices. Thank you for giving me wisdom to know the difference. I declare that I will receive strength from your Word to stand strong in midst of temptation. I will not knowingly cause my brother or sister to go astray. I will call upon your name daily and expect deliverance.

Reading & Meditation:
"If any of you lack wisdom, let him ask of god, that giveth to all men liberally, and upbraideth not; and it shall be given him. But let him ask in faith, nothing wavering..."
(James 1:5-6 KJV)

But every man is tempted when he is drawn away of his own lust, and enticed. (James 1:14 KJV)

"Be ye therefore followers of God..." (Ephesians 5:1 KJV)

"...We ought to obey God rather than men." (Acts 5:29 KJV)

If we confess our sins, he is faithful and just to forgive us our sins, and to cleanse us from all unrighteousness.
(I John 1:9 KJV)

Call unto me, and I will answer thee, and show thee great and mighty things, which thou knowest not. (Jeremiah 33:3 KJV)

He that causeth the righteous to go astray in an evil way, he shall fall himself into his own pit: but the upright shall have good things in possession. (Proverbs 28:10 KJV)

"...work out your own salvation with fear and trembling."
(Philippians 2:12 KJV)

"See, I have set before thee this day life and good, and death and evil..." (Deuteronomy 30:15 KJV)

"...but they measuring themselves by themselves, and comparing themselves among themselves, are not wise..." (2 Corinthians 10:12 KJV)

Journal
Keep Your Eyes Off Church People

Are You A Runner?

Anyone who does not have rule over their own spirit is like a city in ruin, with no walls [regulations]. The stability of this type of city is questionable at best. Anything and anybody can enter and exit at will. We can expect to be in this condition, if we don't regulate, direct and control what goes into and out of our spirit. God is a Spirit. As Believers, we are required to worship Him in Spirit and in truth. When your spirit is not being regulated, you will find yourself fleeing when no one is pursuing you. Some people run from church to church trying to find a comfortable place for their flesh to rest, or they run from city to city trying to find the most prominent church to teach, counsel others or display their talents. Refusal to regulate anger, bitterness, rejection, pride, disobedience; all these will cause people to run from place to place. There is no rest for the spirit that is without regulation.

In some ways, a runner is not much different than a drug abuser or an alcoholic. In the hopes of a quick escape from what hurts, the drugs and alcohol send them to places that temporarily mask their pain. Have church people caused you pain, discomfort or embarrassment? I am a witness to how it hurts, but you can pass over the transgression. Stability is important. Although it is sometimes necessary, the answer is not always to pack up and move on. Before deciding, consider this: How big is your God? Can he do everything except change a person's heart, deal with those who have hurt you, or reveal your gifts and talents? Did you expect someone to be at another level in their faith, and they let you down? Have you made an honest effort to work through the conflict you've encountered? Why should God do anything about these matters if you run? This could be the season when God is pressing you to grow, and pressure is always unpleasant.

People who wander and roam are untrustworthy. They may not stay that way, but while they are on the move they may not be good ministry material because their commitment is questionable. An offense of any magnitude might cause them to jump ship.

In my earlier years, I remember searching for a place to worship. I was never connected to any local group of Believers for more than a few years. My desire was not to be unstable; but because I had a zeal that was not according to knowledge, I was always on the move. I wanted to eat meat when I needed milk. But God honored my persistent desire to know Him. I let offenses manipulate my character and was often unforgiving of others. Some years later, after I suffered some things, I allowed the Word of God to settle within me and started trusting God.

But let's just say you've decided to leave anyway. You've been offended, and you refuse to take it anymore! If God will forgive and cleanse a person from the most horrendous sin imaginable, then certainly you can be forgiven for the inability of your heart (lack of faith) to withstand the offense that you believe was initiated against you.

Not everyone separates from a church because of an offense. Some leave in search of a more convenient location, changing cities, looking for different ministry activities, etc. I will not condone or discredit any of these reasons, because we are all individual free-will moral agents of the choices that we make. Consider this: could it be that you are the one God wants to stand in the gap and pray the prayer of faith over situations that he has allowed you to see?

Wherever you were born again or reconciled from backsliding, settle down and let God cultivate your life in that place. Refuse to be ungrateful and selfish, or to quickly run away with your prayers and help in your bosom, because of an uncomfortable situation. Remember, you have caused some uncomfortable offenses also. So, let your prayers come up as a memorial unto your God for your leaders and fellow Believers. Expect God to answer you. He is a great God.

Strength for the Journey

Affirmation:
I declare I will stand firm through offense and any other attack that threatens to shift my focus or shake my faith. I will be slow to anger and quick to forgive.

Reading & Meditation:
He that hath no rule over his own spirit is like a city that is broken down, and without walls. (Proverbs 25:28 KJV)

God is a Spirit: and they that worship him must worship him in spirit and in truth. (John 4:24 KJV)

And I will set my face against you, and ye shall be slain before your enemies: they that hate you shall reign over you; and ye shall flee when none pursueth you. (Isaiah 26:17 KJV);

'The wicked flee when no one pursueth..." (Proverbs 28:1 KJV)

He that is slow to anger is better than the mighty; and he that ruleth his spirit than he that taketh a city. (Proverbs 16:32 KJV)

The discretion of a man deferreth his anger; and it is his glory to pass over a transgression. (Proverbs 19:11 KJV)

As a bird that wandereth from her nest, so is a man that wandereth from his place. (Proverbs 27:8 KJV)

"Thus saith the LORD unto this people, Thus have they loved to wander, they have not refrained their feet, therefore the LORD doth not accept them..." (Jeremiah 14:10 KJV)

But God is the judge: he putteth down one, and setteth up another. (Psalms 75:7 KJV)

For as the heavens are higher than the earth, so are my ways higher than your ways, and my thoughts than your thoughts. (Isaiah 55:9 KJV)

"With him is an arm of flesh; but with us is the LORD our God to help us, and to fight our battles..." (2 Chronicles 32:8 KJV)

"Thus saith the LORD; Cursed be the man that trusteth in man, and maketh flesh his arm..." (Jeremiah 17:5 KJV)

And he shall be like a tree planted by the rivers of water, that bringeth forth his fruit in his season; his leaf also shall not wither; and whatsoever he doeth shall prosper. (Psalms 1:3 KJV)

And when ye stand praying, forgive, if you have ought against any: that your Father also which is in heaven may forgive you your trespasses. But if ye do not forgive, neither will your Father which is in heaven forgive your trespasses. (Mark 11:25-26 KJV)

And I sought for a man among them, that should makeup the hedge, and stand in the gap before me for the land, that I should not destroy it: but I found none. (Ezekiel 22:30 KJV)

"Be still and know that I am God..." (Psalms 46:10 KJV)

Journal
Are You A Runner?

Order In The Court!

When a person goes to the court concerning a matter that cannot be resolved without Judicial Intervention, there is an order or proper protocol that must be followed before entering the courtroom. As part of that protocol, a person will probably receive written notification from a liaison (advocate or middleman) of the courts, informing them of what is about to happen and a general expectation of the outcome. They are given instructions on what to wear and what not to wear. They are told when to speak, when not to speak, and what tone to use when a response is requested. They are told where to sit and notified from the beginning to remain in this "in order" status until the judge calls for the case, listens to their side, makes his final and binding decision concerning the matter, and they are dismissed from the courtroom. If that order is not followed, the individual is not in right standing with the judge, who is recognized as the ultimate authority concerning the case, and he will not hear it. If someone is unprepared in one or more areas, the judge may instruct them to come back when the requirements to stand before him have been met.

You may be wondering what all this has to do with offenses in the church. Well, God has a specific protocol that He wants followed before we can enter His Courts. In the Old Testament, priests were instantly killed, if they did not enter the presence of God by following the protocol. For Believers, Jesus is our liaison, and He has delivered to us written instructions from God concerning how we should enter His Courts. When we come before the Almighty Father God requesting help for a matter that cannot be resolved without divine intervention, the order in which we must enter God's presence is with clean hands and heart; coming before Him with a broken (humble) and contrite (penitent, remorseful) spirit. The prelude for many worship services take on this order. When we enter the church, expecting to receive the answers that we need, reverence and respect for God's presence should be paramount. The time for prayer and cleansing of hearts and minds should not be commingled with fellowship and frolicking. This observation is not a critique, but rather an exhortation to a higher level of excellence and obedience. If we don't enter His courts correctly, God can refuse to answer just because we are out of order or being disrespectful toward those who may already be in His presence. Although they may never tell you, it is incredibly offensive to people, whose trials and tribulations are pressing them, that (during their time of prayer, cleansing and honoring God's presence) individuals are causing distractions. For example: refusing to be easily entreated when different matters are addressed with diplomacy. Yes, the Lord has instructed us to come boldly to His throne of grace to obtain help when we need it; but we boldly go because we know we have entered His Gates and Courts correctly. If this step is skipped, we have come into the Courts of God unprepared, half dressed, or without the proper attire, which may affect the outcome of our petitions.

Many churches have a designated time at the beginning of their worship services for exhortation, encouraging the congregation to stay focused on its purpose of ministering to God before He ministers to us. The order of service also includes time to praise, to sing, and dance before the Lord, and to offer expressions of adoration, devotion, honor, worship, applause, rejoicing and glory. There is even a time for laughter in the church. Every congregation has a specific order that they follow, but the proper way to enter God's Courts is the same. As true worshipers of God, we must remain in this "in order status" continually in our day-to-day lives until we are dismissed from this earth. God's instructions are not tedious or restricting; they are for our benefit. If we love God, we will willingly follow them.

Most people are willing to follow the instructions of the court systems, the attorneys and the judges to the letter; they make an effort not to enter the courtroom incorrectly and unprepared because they are expecting a favorable outcome. I believe that, as Believers, we should make a greater effort to reverence the House of God and His presence, exalting Him higher than our earthly authorities. Our government was placed upon His shoulder; He is the Judge of all judges; our Wonderful Counselor; the King of Kings and Lord of Lords. He is the Great I AM. Enter His gates with thanksgiving and courts with praise. Respect God's order and come boldly expecting to see the hand of the Lord in healing and deliverance, as the Glory of God falls upon the congregation. Expect to activate the favor of God upon your life because you love and honor His Word.

Strength for the Journey

Affirmation:
I will prepare my heart, mind, and my tongue for worship. I will check my attitude and consider my motives before I raise my hands in worship.

Reading & Meditation:
"...Nadab and Abihu, however, fell dead before the LORD when they made an offering with unauthorized fire before him in the Desert of Sinai..." (Numbers 3:4 NIV)

"Be careful what you do when you go to the temple of God; draw near to listen rather than to offer a sacrifice like fools, for they do not realize that they are doing wrong. 2 Do not be rash with your mouth or hasty in your heart to bring up a matter before God..." (Eccl 5:1 KJV)

All scripture is given by inspiration of God, and is profitable for doctrine, for reproof, for correction, for instruction in righteousness:" (II Timothy 3:16 KJV)

Enter into his gates with thanksgiving, and into his courts with praise: be thankful unto him, and bless his name. (Psalms 100:4 KJV)

Create in me a clean heart, O God; and renew a right spirit within me. (Psalms 51:10 KJV)

He that hath clean hands, and a pure heart; who hath not lifted up his soul unto vanity, nor sworn deceitfully. He shall receive the blessing from the LORD, and righteousness from the God of his salvation. (Psalms 24:4-5 KJV)

"Draw nigh unto God, and he will draw nigh to you. Cleanse your hands, ye sinners; and purify your hearts, ye double minded... Humble yourselves in the sight of the Lord, and he shall lift you up." (James 4:8; 4:10 KJV)

The LORD is nigh unto them that are of a broken heart; and saveth such as be of a contrite spirit. (Psalms 34:18 KJV)

Let us therefore come boldly unto the throne of grace, that we may obtain mercy, and find grace to help in time of need. (Hebrews 4:16 KJV)

Wherefore God also hath highly exalted him, and given him a name which is above every name: That at the name of Jesus every knee should bow, of things in heaven, and things in earth, and things under the earth; And that every tongue should confess that Jesus Christ is Lord, to the glory of God the Father. (Philippians 2:9-11 KJV)

For unto us a child is born, unto us a son is given: and the government shall be upon his shoulder: and his name shall be called Wonderful, Counsellor, The mighty God, The everlasting Father, The Prince of Peace. (Isaiah 9:6 KJV)

"...What is his name?" "... And God said unto Moses, I AM THAT I AM..." (Exodus 3:13-14 KJV)

Journal
Order In The Court

From the Author

Have you been praying for something specific for a long time and still waiting for the answer? There are many reasons answers to prayers appear to be delayed. If your request lines up with the Word of God, the answer is never: No. God answers yes, but maybe the person he chose to bring the solution to you is struggling to obey and is out of place; so, God must raise up someone else for the task. Tangible blessings and answers to prayers don't magically fall out of the sky. God needs to use a human being willing to be a vessel or a conduit to get it to you. Undoubtedly, you (or someone you know) experienced church hurt at some point or you wouldn't be reading this book. If you are thinking of a situation where you received an offense, and it is still bothersome, then you haven't released it. Holding on to an offense, for any reason, will block the answer to your prayers.

Church hurt is a tool the enemy uses to frustrate the Believer's faith, but it is within your power to disarm him. The next two volumes of this series are vital to your success. Be sure to journal your thoughts and, and pray about them. Practice forgiving others and forgiving yourself. I am in expectation of your testimony on how you recovered from church hurt, and I rejoice with you in advance!

Strength for the Journey

Affirmation:
I am strong in the Lord and in the power of His might. I have the mind of Christ. I am able to apply God's Word to my situation and quickly recover from church hurt.

Reading & Meditation:
"And the times of this ignorance God winked at; but now commandeth all men every where to repent..." (Acts 17:30)

Blessed is the man that endureth temptations: for when he is tried, he shall receive the crown of life, which the Lord hath promised to them that love him. (James 1:12);

Submit yourselves therefore to God. Resist the devil, and he will flee from you. (James 4:7)

Nay, in all these things we are more than conquerors through him that loved us. (Romans 8:37)

Let us therefore come boldly unto the throne of grace, that we may obtain mercy, and find grace to help in time of need. (Hebrews 4:16)

And we know that all things work together for good to them that love God, to them who are the called according to his purpose. (Romans 8:28)

Journal
What decisions have you made?
What changes will you make?

_____

_____

_____

_____

_____

_____

_____

_____

_____

_____

_____

_____

_____

_____

_____

_____

_____

_____

_____

_____

_____

_____

_____

_____

_____

_____

They Call It Church Hurt

Read the Entire Series

Vol 1 – Church People
Why Fellowship?
A Brother Offended, A Sister Offended
Are You A Fighter?
Is Your Struggle With People?
Keep Your Eyes Off Church People
Are You A Runner?
Order In The Court

Vol 2 – Growing Pains
Learning to Trust God
What About My Reputation?
Mount Up With Wings As Eagles & Get Over It
Why So Down Cast, Oh My Soul?
Guard Your Heart
Jealousy Has Many Faces
Ordinary Just Won't Do

Vol 3 – Attitude & Perspective
The Members of the Clergy
Another Sheep Has Left the Fold
Unfaithful & Untrustworthy
Money Matters & Relationships
Forgive Me, My Plate is Full
Calculated Offenses

Strength For The Journey
Journal

October Day Publishing
www.octoberdaypublishing.pub